This 1751 painting of West Wycombe Park, Buckinghamshire, by John Hannan shows a massive rocky arch above a reclining river god, with water dashing over the weir to the River Wye below.

Fountains
and Water Features

Rosalind Hopwood

A Shire book

2

Published in 2004 by Shire Publications Ltd,
Cromwell House, Church Street, Princes Risborough,
Buckinghamshire HP27 9AA, UK.
(Website: www.shirebooks.co.uk)

Copyright © 2004 by Rosalind Hopwood.
First published 2004.
Shire Album 435. ISBN 0 7478 0607 1.
Rosalind Hopwood is hereby identified as the author of
this work in accordance with Section 77 of the Copyright,
Designs and Patents Act 1988.

British Library Cataloguing in Publication Data:
Hopwood, Rosalind
Fountains and water features. – (Shire album; 435)
1. Water in landscape architecture
2. Water in landscape architecture – Pictorial works
3. Fountains
4. Fountains – Pictorial works
I. Title 714
ISBN 0 7478 0607 1.

Cover: *The 'Atlas' fountain at Castle Howard, North Yorkshire, sculpted by John Thomas, was erected in 1853. Atlas, lord of the earth's furthest shores and of the seas that receive the setting sun, was condemned to support the globe of the heavens for eternity.*

Printed in Malta by Gutenberg Press Limited, Gudja Road,
Tarxien PLA 19, Malta

Contents

A modern presentation of moving water at Kiftsgate Court in Gloucestershire, where a computer program controls the flow of water from gold-plated casts of philodendron leaves. Designed by Simon Allison in 2001.

Early fountains

It is held by physicists and philosophers and priests that all things in life depend on the power of water... For it is the chief requisite of life, for happiness and everyday life.
(Vitruvius, *The Ten Books on Architecture* VIII, 31–27 BC)

The water features covered in this introduction to fountain evolution take many forms, including natural springs, *jets d'eau* (water jets), rills and cascades, and all incorporate moving water. Still water features are excluded. The word 'fountain' comes from the Latin term *fons*, meaning 'source', and may represent a natural spring or the actual jet or spray of water. A fountain may be a simple basin or an ornamental structure from which water emerges in a variety of artistic shapes.

Water features within architectural structures probably originated in Greece and Asia Minor when springs were enclosed to preserve their purity and were later decorated as shrines. The cities of ancient Roman times had aqueducts in stone-cut or brick-built channels above or below the ground and Vitruvius, writing in the first century BC, suggested a 6 inch slope per 100 feet (152 mm per 30 metres) to provide the gradient necessary for water flow. To traverse valleys, aqueducts were built on arched bridges, or inverted siphon systems were made of interlocking lead pipes, their bends strengthened by being set in *pozzolana*, a type of cement that helped withstand the pressure of the water. Vitruvius and, in the first century AD, Pliny the Elder described *pozzolana* as a mix of limestone, sand, small stone debris and volcanic dust from around Mount Vesuvius that solidified under water.

The aqueducts fed reservoirs and water-towers and the water then moved on to smaller holding tanks for public use. Pliny the Elder in his

The lead pipes possibly dating from the sixteenth century at the Villa Medici, at Castello near Florence, are constructed according to Pliny the Elder's advice, with the pipes slotted together to feed the grotto fountains below.

Natural Histories tells us how lead pipes were made from 10 foot (3 metre) lengths that were shaped and overlapped around a wooden former and then slotted together. Bronze, wood and terracotta pipes lined with quicklime and oil were also used in cities.

Fountains in private gardens such as those at Pompeii were usually placed against a wall, with a concealed raised cistern fed by rainwater from the roof of the building. Pliny the Elder reminded engineers that water will rise only as high as its source, and that if a jet were required the primary source would have to be much higher than the fountain. He also recommended that fountain pipes should be of bronze, with the down-pipe diameter three times that of the up-pipe to ensure a forceful jet of water.

The only pump used in Roman times to be described by Vitruvius was a small cylinder pump dating from the third century BC and invented by Ctesibius of Alexandria. It was a force pump with two vertical cylinders and bronze pistons that worked reciprocally on a rocker arm, but this was suitable only for a small fountain. Such pumps were later used during the early Renaissance period. Tread-wheels and buckets on chains raised water for services such as the public baths in Pompeii but large urban fountains usually had a continuous flow of water feeding a public outlet and onwards into the sewers.

Vitruvius also reported on the hydraulic texts of Philo of Byzantium in the second century BC and Heron of Alexandria in the first century AD that described piston pumps, siphons, valve controls and trick fountains, later known as *giochi d'aqua*. The Romans enjoyed ingenious water features and during the first century AD Pliny the Younger described one in the form of a carved couch, the cushion of which had water spouting from its corners. Much fountain decoration was inspired by Greek and Roman pagan mythology, especially by Ovid's *Metamorphoses*, also dating from the early first century AD.

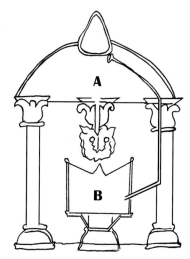

Lion masks were one of the earliest forms of waterspout. This fountain by Philo, dating from between 250 and 200 BC, shows a trick wall fountain. Liquid was poured into Chamber A and sealed. The outlet at the base allowed liquid to flow out through the mask and into B. The flow depended on the level of liquid in B. If the liquid covered the return pipe a vacuum would eventually be formed in A, stopping the flow of liquid. If liquid was removed from B, exposing the pipe, the vacuum was broken and the flow restarted. In this fountain wine was used.

A quarter of a million gallons of water bubble up daily through a fault below the city of Bath in Somerset, appearing at the Roman Baths. The water comes from the Mendip Hills. The decorative overflow arch above the thermal spring, which rises at 46 degrees centigrade, marks the importance this water had to the Romans. The water channel is stained red by the many minerals.

From earliest times the Romans venerated water, often described in their texts as a gift from the gods. The appearance and movement of water by an unseen power led to offerings being placed at the water source. Similar rituals took place in Britain in the 70s AD, when a temple was built to Sulis Minerva beside the sacred spring at Bath in Somerset. Roman offerings were later found in this sacred pool.

By the eighth century a mix of Islamic and Persian garden styles had spread into Spain. By the thirteenth century the Alhambra Palace in Granada included water features based on the Persian concept of the three states of water – a bubbling spout, a shallow sheet of moving water and a still pool. The Arab writer Al Jazarì in the thirteenth century recorded various hydraulic devices, including the tipping

Below: *Four rills (stone-lined channels holding running water) traverse the Court of the Lions in the Alhambra Palace, Granada, Spain, with the central fountain basin supported on the backs of twelve lions that spout water. In antiquity water was used to keep insects at bay, temper the air and muffle conversations.*

This fountain at Kiftsgate Court, Gloucestershire, illustrates the type of carved decoration used during medieval times to show the Labours of the Months, with the grape harvest in autumn.

fountain. These early devices, together with those of Philo and Heron, would become the pattern book for the hydraulic automata of Renaissance fountains.

Water plays a central role in many religions – from the rivers in the Garden of Eden to the fountains of the Koran. When the Arab hordes overran the old Persian Empire during the seventh century they found the 'fountains gushing with water' in the 'Paradise gardens' described in the Koran. Later, in the thirteenth century, some Christian fonts were decorated with the Labours of the Months, and civic fountains with religious and civic imagery.

In Britain a medieval water feature known as Rosamund's Bower was built around 1165 for 'Fair Rosamund' Clifford, mistress of King Henry II, and by

The Fontana Maggiore in Perugia, Italy, dating from 1278, is adorned with religious, civic and traditional decoration to celebrate the prestige of the city. It is built in pink-and-white marble, with three bronze water-carriers at the apex marking the arrival of water from a new aqueduct.

The natural spring in Rosamund's Bower at Blenheim Palace, Oxfordshire, was known as 'Everswell' and is probably the oldest designed water feature in Britain. A tranquil retreat known as a 'pleasance' was based around this font or spring.

This 1986 reconstruction in Queen Eleanor's Garden, Winchester, has four bronze leopard-head spouts jetting water into the octagonal basin. Like the Alhambra Palace fountain, this one too is linked to a rill. The bronze falcon on an orb is a copy from a choir stall dating from 1305 in Winchester Cathedral.

the thirteenth century records in Britain described simple stand fountains. A reconstructed fountain in Queen Eleanor's Garden at Winchester is based on a 1270s description of a fountain in Charing Cross Mews, Westminster. Medieval texts such as Crescenzi's *De vegetabilibus et plantis* (1304–9) encouraged the inclusion of a fountain in a garden, and medieval romances such as the Flemish *Roman de la Rose* from the thirteenth century centred on a Fountain of Love.

The fifteenth-century discovery of ancient texts led to a renewal of artistic and technological interest in fountain construction, although in Italy wall fountains remained the most common type. The bronze *Winged Boy with a Fantastic Fish*, now in the Victoria and Albert Museum in London, is an early example. During the early Renaissance water supply to fountains was intermittent, so the fountain also needed visual impact to hold the attention of the viewer. This viewing problem was solved when the lost-wax method of bronze casting was revived from antiquity and freestanding figures could be produced. By the 1480s Italian masters such as Verrocchio were making

'Winged Boy with a Fantastic Fish', probably by Donatello in the 1430s, may have sprayed his own water upwards on to a water-wheel on a rod held in his right hand, while the fish over his shoulder spouted water. Water entered through a hole in the back of the figure.

small bronze freestanding fountains for wealthy patrons as pleasure fountains and to display the patron's interests and prestige. Fountain basins standing on a stem in this way are known as 'cyclix' fountains because they resemble a classical drinking cup.

However, hydraulic technology was still basic. Vitruvius' manuscript had been discovered in 1408, prompting new interest in hydraulics. Mariano Taccola, an engineer from Siena, in the 1430s illustrated and briefly explained ancient devices, re-worked but not improved. Man and animal power worked huge vertical wheels with buckets and boxes attached to

This copy of Verrocchio's bronze sculpture of 'Putto with a Dolphin' from the 1480s stands in the courtyard of the Palazzo Vecchio in Florence. Lost-wax bronze casting begins with the coating of a plaster model in wax, which is then surrounded by a casing of rough material called 'scrim'. After the wax has been melted out, the resulting void is filled with molten bronze. When the piece has been fired the casing and the core are removed and finally the bronze is chased to a high sheen.

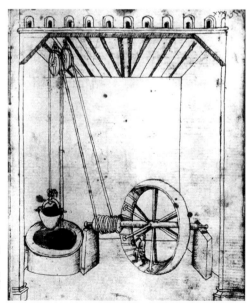

In 1433 Taccola illustrated the tread-wheel, a wooden device up to 14 feet (4 metres) in diameter. It was worked by manpower to raise water to a height at which, in this case, it could be decanted to fill a cistern and so feed a wall fountain.

In 'Hypnerotomachia Poliphili', water jetting from the breasts of the Three Graces symbolised benevolence. Water circulated through the heads of the dragons and out through the lion masks into the receiving basin before returning to the cornucopias, or horns of plenty, at the top, which also jetted water.

them that dipped into a low water source. Some examples indicated the necessity of a raised water source and others showed Taccola's ideas of a working piston pump.

New interest in designs arose in 1499 with the publication in Venice of *Hypnerotomachia Poliphili* by Francesco Colonna. Poliphilo, the hero, journeys through a dream garden that is decorated with allegorical fountains, such as the gilded *Three Graces* fountain. The *Fountain of Mirth* amuses and provokes interest in hydraulics when, in the sculpture, a boy sprays his own water into the face of Poliphilo. Earlier, in 1485, Leon Battista Alberti had declared in *De re aedifactoria* that he did not disapprove of comic fountains provided they were not obscene.

'Giochi d'aqua' were popular with visitors in the heat of the day in Italy, but less so in the colder climates of northern Europe. These seventeenth-century 'giochi d'aqua' at the Villa Barbarigo at Valsanzebio in Italy would originally have been activated by hand from a nearby stopcock. Movement detectors now activate them.

The fountain at Linlithgow Palace, West Lothian, is in the shape of a closed crown and represents the supreme power of the king, James V of Scotland. Water from the carved sun on the underside of the upper crown fell through eight animal heads to the middle basin, representing the bounty of God and the king. Water probably came from an underground aqueduct near the walls.

The sixteenth and seventeenth centuries

Sixteenth-century travellers returned to Britain with descriptions of European water features that could be adapted to suit the requirements of British taste. The oldest surviving fountain in Britain is the Linlithgow fountain, West Lothian, built for King James V of Scotland in about 1538. The local sandstone used would have been easily worked, but after exposure to the elements the sandstone has eroded and is undergoing restoration. This fountain ran with wine to celebrate the visit of Charles Edward Stewart to Linlithgow in 1745. A copy of the fountain was made for Linlithgow Cross after 1660 to celebrate the return of King Charles II to the throne, and parts of this were later integrated into the base of the central fountain at Pitmedden, Aberdeenshire.

By 1543 the humanist Claudio Tolomei, writing in Rome, mentioned the potential for fountain design and noted 'the ingenious artifice recently rediscovered to make the fountains just seen, [that] was used long ago in Rome'. Renaissance patrons commissioned their own fountains with allegorical references for propaganda purposes. A good

Above: The base of the fountain at Pitmedden, Aberdeenshire, is inscribed with a partly illegible date from the seventeenth century. Water sprays into the hexagonal pool from carved balusters with animal and angel-head decoration and from animal heads on urns.

In the garden of the Villa Medici at Castello, Florence, the bronze figure of Venus or Florence (sometimes called either), completed by Giambologna in 1572, wrings water from her hair, portraying the goddess who rose from the sea. It implies that the fertility of the city is a result of the unification of the local rivers at this fountain, thanks to the magnanimity of Duke Cosimo I de' Medici.

De Caus's drawing is similar to the 'Mount Parnassus' fountain built in the garden of Somerset House, London, which would have been crowned by the horse Pegasus stamping to release the font of the Muses, implying that poetry and the arts flourished at the queen's court. The fountain was at least 80 feet (24 metres) in diameter.

example is the fountain of *Florence* in the Medici gardens at Castello near Florence. This is a 'candelabrum' fountain, so called because the central shaft stands in a large receiving basin and carries multiple basins surmounted by a statue.

In 1609 Salomon de Caus, author of *Les Raisons des Eaux Mouvants* (1615), came to work for Queen Anne, wife of James I, at Somerset House in London. Following the Italian trend for allegory and invention, he designed the *Mount Parnassus* fountain, representing the scene from Ovid's *Metamorphoses* in which the sacred font of the Muses was created. During 1579 Giambologna had devised a similar fountain-grotto, called *Appennino,* at the Villa Demidoff at Pratolino in Italy; methods of cementing the many materials used in its construction are not

The giant 'Appennino' at the Villa Demidoff, Pratolino, is about 35 feet (11 metres) high and is made of brick and stone with mossy encrustations of tufa (a volcanic rock) and tartar to give a weathered appearance. The giant presses down on the head of a monster to release water. As a personification of the nearby mountains, it symbolises the source of water for the gardens.

Above left: The 'Venus' fountain at Bolsover Castle, Derbyshire, in pink-and-white limestone with black-and-white marble figures. In the antique style, 'putti' (little boys in ancient mythology) enliven the fountain by adding their own sprays of water as a symbol of good luck while lustful beasts look on.

Above right: The 'Arethusa' fountain, in the traditional materials of bronze and stone, designed by Inigo Jones and renamed the 'Diana' fountain, stands in a 400 foot (122 metre) diameter pool in Bushy Park, having been moved here from Hampton Court Palace at the beginning of King George III's reign. The nymph Arethusa inspired pastoral poetry, one of the interests of the queen's court.

recorded but it is most likely that *pozzolana* was used. By 1659 Isaac de Caus, nephew of Salomon, considered cement-making in his book *New and Rare Inventions of Water Works*. He suggested a mixture of ground glass, linseed oil and slaked lime, holding that 'it will not be moistened in any way'.

In 1613 the Italianate style of formal fountain gardens had been noted by Gervase Markham in *The English Husbandman* when he suggested a 'conduit of antic fashion' – a 'conduit' being any feature of moving water. However, before such grand water gardens became fashionable in Britain, smaller courtly gardens associated with poetry and love made pleasant retreats. William Cavendish, Earl of Newcastle, who created his own garden at Bolsover Castle in Derbyshire, took up the idea. Around 1628 local craftsmen made a fountain in the walled garden, copied from the Venus figure by Giambologna now at the Pitti Palace in Florence. King Charles I and Queen Henrietta Maria went to Bolsover in 1634 to be entertained by a masque by Ben Jonson called *Love's Welcome to Bolsover*.

References to the courtly life of Queen Henrietta Maria appear in the *Arethusa* fountain commissioned from Hubert le Sueur for Somerset House between 1635 and 1637. Originally the basin of black marble was adorned by a bronze female figure, four sirens astride dolphins and aquatic decoration. In 1655 the Lord Protector Oliver Cromwell had the

The Privy Garden at Hampton Court Palace was restored during the early 1990s to its original plan of 1701. The central basin marks the original position of the 'Arethusa' fountain, placed here from its assembly in 1655–6 until 1691, after which it was refurbished with Portland stone to replace the black marble and re-sited in 1701, again within the Privy Garden.

fountain removed from Somerset House and placed in the centre of the Privy Garden at Hampton Court Palace.

The Venus figure that was so popular in Italy appears indoors at Chatsworth House in Derbyshire, where the marble *Toilet of Venus* decorates the wall fountain of the interior grotto. The sculpture was bought in 1692 for £16 and set above a trough of local black Ashford marble. Another Italian delight included at Chatsworth in 1692 was an example of *giochi d'aqua* or trick fountains, already known from travellers abroad and from translations of Francesco Colonna's *Hypnerotomachia Poliphili* into French (1546) and English (1592).

The 'Toilet of Venus' fountain in the grotto at Chatsworth House, Derbyshire, carved in high relief, was framed in limestone by local craftsmen and carved with aquatic imagery and dolphins.

Hydraulics moved on apace when in 1696 Carlo Fontana wrote *The Most Useful Treatise on Moving Waters: Its Movement through Conduits* and in the same year the French artist Grillet was called in to design the grand sparkling *Cascade* at Chatsworth House. A reservoir on the north-eastern moors supplies water by gravity to the *Cascade* on the sloping east front, which in turn feeds the *Sea-Horse and Triton* fountain. Made of stone, this fountain was carved from 1688 to 1691 by the Danish sculptor Caius Gabriel Cibber and, despite weathering, the prancing sea-horses still toss their heads and coil their fishy tails in vigorous twisting poses.

Above: *The copper and lead 'Willow Tree' fountain at Chatsworth House, now in the Rock Garden, sprays water from its branches and leaves. Originally from 1692, it has been replaced twice and was repaired in 1842 by Paxton, who reassembled the eight thousand pieces to feed eight hundred jets. Princess Victoria described it as the 'squirting tree'.*

Right: *At Chatsworth House the 'Cascade' has water flowing over twenty-four groups of steps in various sizes to produce differing aural tones. On the roof of the Cascade House, added by Thomas Archer in 1703, a sleeping river god reclines between river nymphs as dolphins coil down columns decorated with frost-work to jet water into the cascade.*

The literary source for the imagery of the 'Sea-Horse and Triton' fountain at Chatsworth House is Ovid's 'Metamorphoses', Book I: 'Then he called to the sea-god Triton, who rose from the deep...Neptune bade him blow on his echoing conch shell...all the waves which heard it were checked in their course...'.

The Great Fountain Garden at Hampton Court Palace, originally laid out by Daniel Marot in 1701, now has a central fountain with either a 'jet d'eau' (a single vertical jet of water) or a crown effect of sprayed water.

The eighteenth century

During the eighteenth century the general interest in fountains collapsed. The change in the monarchy in 1689 led to the introduction of Dutch garden styles and to the later introduction of the English landscape style of gardening from the mid eighteenth century. Only the outline of one formal fountain garden from the reign of William and Mary remains, at Hampton Court Palace, laid out in 1701 by the Frenchman Daniel Marot. Thirteen fountains were arranged in a semicircular parterre (an ornamental design of plants), called the Grand Fountain Garden, on the east front. Re-siting and remodelling of fountains became easier as British engineers learned from continental experts such as the Florentine Francini brothers working at Versailles for King Louis XIV in the 1680s.

Some landowners, such as Thomas Coke, Vice Chamberlain to King William III and owner of Melbourne Hall in Derbyshire, preferred to design their own water features. After studying in France, Coke consulted the royal gardeners London and Wise and began work at Melbourne in 1704. The piped water supply for fountains in the wooded garden and the yew walk came by gravity feed from

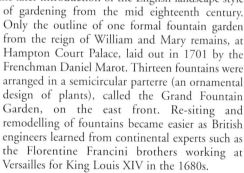

Within the yew walk at Melbourne Hall, Derbyshire, statues of putti spray jets from fish to add sparkle to the dim interior. A chain of pools with bubble fountains was also installed in the woodland walk when the garden was designed.

The 'Dragon Cascade' at Bramham Park from the early eighteenth century has not changed since Zeigler's painting of 1825. This fountain, like the one below, has a shaped basin and rusticated (rough) stonework decoration.

a mill pool above the garden. George Sorocold, the hydraulic engineer concerned, raised the water-level to give added pressure but unfortunately flooded the nearby vicarage garden!

Returning from his grand tour in 1697, Robert Benson, the first Lord Bingley, redesigned his garden at Bramham Park in West Yorkshire between 1710 and 1728. Five pools are constructed in the local limestone and are supplied by gravity flow from local springs. The garden represents the overlapping period between formal designs and the newly fashionable landscape style. Dézallier d'Argenville's *Theory and Practice of Gardening* (1709) and Bernard Bélidor's four volumes on hydraulics (1737–53) became increasingly popular in France, where fountains were the most important feature of gardens, but in Britain the formal style was waning and the pastoral style took over.

At Bramham Park, West Yorkshire, a dragon-mask fountain connects the basins of the Octagonal Pool and Obelisk Pond, leading to a water chute (a low-stepped cascade).

Water patters down Drum Fall to the canal at Studley Royal, North Yorkshire, and surges over the man-made cascade, flanked by two ornate piers and fishing pavilions.

As the English landscape style gathered momentum patrons turned their attention to cascades instead of fountains. John Aislabie's water garden at Studley Royal in North Yorkshire was created from the River Skell between 1716 and 1730 following Aislabie's resignation as Chancellor of the Exchequer after the scandal of the South Sea Bubble. Cascades became fashionable water features and by 1730 the longest and tallest cascade, of twenty-one varied steps, had been built at Stanway in Gloucestershire.

In 1728 Robert Castell's book *The Villas of the Ancients* described contemporary thinking on the landscape style, citing Pliny the Younger's garden as 'a painted scene'. Possibly with this in mind, Francis Dashwood returned from Italy in 1735

The cascade at Stanway House, Gloucestershire, made of Cotswold stone, is fed from the Upper Pond and falls over a rock-work waterfall and irregular stones to produce varied water flow. In 2004 the cascade was undergoing restoration. The jet d'eau was also renovated, making this the tallest known gravity-fed garden fountain.

Replacing the grotto archway of earlier years, water splashes and surges over the angular stones set on the cascade at West Wycombe Park, Buckinghamshire.

Right: *At Harewood House in West Yorkshire the head gardener constructed a regularly stepped cascade before 'Capability' Brown could modify the grounds into a more natural style in 1772.*

The stream in Windsor Great Park called Virginia Water was dammed in 1749 to create a lake for William Augustus, Duke of Cumberland. King George IV later used the lake for fishing. In 1782 this cascade, constructed from boulders from Bagshot Heath, replaced the original.

The 'Sleeping Nymph' was possibly one of the first antique statues to be transformed into a fountain, in 1512 in the Vatican Belvedere in Rome. Here in the grotto at Stourhead, Wiltshire, a copy 'sleeps' above the rising springs that feed the garden. In the 1790s Lady Anne Hadaway wrote that 'the waters tinkling round her…have an effect that is pleasingly melancholy'.

and redesigned his property at West Wycombe Park, Buckinghamshire. The River Wye was dammed to make an octagonal lake and a rocky arch was installed, although by 1781 statues of nymphs on flint piers had replaced the arch (see title page). Other examples at Harewood House in West Yorkshire and Virginia Water in Windsor Great Park illustrate different styles of cascade building.

When they returned from grand tours wealthy patrons often celebrated antiquity in their gardens with relevant water features. At Stourhead, Wiltshire, in 1748 Henry Hoare II had Cheere's lead copy of the *Sleeping Nymph* set above a cold bath fed by a spring; John Evelyn, the traveller and diarist, had seen the original antique sculpture in Rome during 1645. These various fountains and water features met with divided responses, and by 1755 John Shebbeare declared that 'the *jet d'eau* is quite out of fashion in this kingdom… in truth it is always unnatural to see water rising into the air, contrary to its original tendency'.

The nineteenth century

The Industrial Revolution sounded the death knell for the natural landscape style. New technology helped fountains and water features to regain their popularity with far wider accessibility, while mass production of cast iron allowed lower-cost manufacture. Urban populations swelled as country dwellers moved into towns to work in factories, and overcrowding led to concerns about public health. The provision of parks with fountains to recreate the sounds of nature – running water – offered the opportunity to introduce new materials and fountain technology. Private property owners, including the sixth Duke of Devonshire, took advantage of the new technology to install even grander fountains.

Two events in 1851 are worthy of note. First, Hero's *Pneumatica* of AD 62 was republished. It dealt with vacuums, siphons, and valve controls at inlet and outlet points with mechanical starting devices, and laid the foundations for modern hydraulics. Second, the Great Exhibition was held in Joseph Paxton's Crystal Palace at Hyde Park to show the world the artistic and technological prowess of Great Britain. The most striking exhibit was Follett Osler's fountain, made of 4 tons of crystal.

Joseph Paxton installed the gravity-fed 'Emperor' fountain in the canal at Chatsworth House in 1844 for the expected visit of Tsar Nicholas I of Russia. The jet d'eau was at the time the highest gravity-fed garden fountain in the world and has reached 264 feet (81 metres) in height.

Osler's 'Crystal' fountain at the Great Exhibition of 1851. Water arched from two scalloped basins set above crystal parasols and from the apex. The elaborate shaft was supported on cast-iron rods that were invisible to the viewer.

Below: *This cast-iron drinking fountain is from the catalogue of Walter Macfarlane & Company of the Saracen Foundry, Glasgow, from about 1870. There are four basins. Each basin has a tap and a cup hanging by a chain attached to its base. The cup can be inverted to hold water. This particular fountain had the option of a dog trough.*

Water falling 27 feet (8 metres) into the large circular basin reflected light and created rainbow effects through the glittering glass.

Companies offered catalogue selection when fountains were mass-produced in cast iron. Foundries such as Coalbrookdale and Saracen were ready to meet the demands of the government, which passed the Public Health Act in 1875. Concerns about public health were met in part by the provision of public drinking fountains selected from catalogues. Philanthropists such as Frank Crossley, a Yorkshire carpet magnate, funded recreational spaces with fountains for public enjoyment, for example the People's Park in Halifax. Designed by Paxton in 1857, it had 113 *jets d'eau* in a central fountain reaching 50 feet (15 metres). Cast-iron fountains became more widely available as foundries used cheap coal and coke for smelting, instead of charcoal.

In 1851 the Coalbrookdale Company produced the popular cast-iron *Boy and Swan* fountain and soon copies appeared throughout Britain's parks. This versatile and

The original architectural bays flanking the loggia in the People's Park, Halifax, West Yorkshire, have wall fountains, each with four gargoyle heads spurting water downwards into rectangular troughs. In 1914 a marble figure fountain replaced Paxton's original central fountain.

resilient material was manufactured by roasting iron ore in a blast-furnace to purify the metal, with the resulting 'pigs' re-smelted to produce cast iron. Fountain parts were first modelled and then pressed into damp sand to take the shape before the molten metal was poured into the resulting sand mould.

Gifts of civic fountains for public spaces from prosperous benefactors were not always readily accepted. In Edinburgh the *Ross* fountain donated by the gunmaker Daniel Ross in 1864 was not found a home in Princes

Above: *The 'Boy and Swan' fountain as it appeared in the 1851 Coalbrookdale catalogue. At least five copies were made. The jet of water falls over the boy much as in Verrocchio's bronze fountain of the 1480s.*

Right: *This 'Boy and Swan' fountain was returned to the Coalbrookdale Museum, Shropshire, in the 1990s, given a bronzed finish and placed in the grounds. Sculptural detail shows the winged boy gleefully clasping the swan's neck and turning up his toes in an effort to stay upright.*

On the cast-iron 'Ross' fountain in Edinburgh four female figures representing the arts and sciences are seated between semicircular basins. The standing female figure holds a cornucopia (signifying plenty) that sprays water. In order to combat excessive water wastage – which was not resolved until the 1930s – the fountain worked only when the band played.

Right: The 'Saracen' fountain in Alexandra Park, Glasgow, combines classical architecture and Victorian fantasy with sculptures of allegorical females depicting Science, Literature, Commerce and Art. The structure is over 37 feet (11 metres) high and has been refurbished in its original bright colours.

Street Gardens until 1869, and it took two years to find a site in Glasgow for the *Saracen* fountain from the 1901 Glasgow International Exhibition. This and other fountains were used to convey the ethos of Victorian values – for example the *Hitchman* fountain in Leamington Spa commemorated a surgeon who campaigned for the improvement of public health. The *Stewart Memorial* fountain in Glasgow marked the arrival of a supply of clean water from Loch Katrine. Similarly, clean water from the Thirlmere reservoir was commemorated in the *Queen Victoria* Diamond Jubilee fountain, now in Albert Square, Manchester. The fountain, commissioned in 1897 at a cost of £1000, was not universally acclaimed and was described in the press as 'one monument too many'.

Dating from 1897, the 'Queen Victoria' fountain in Manchester is decorated with the arms of the city and of the Duchy of Lancaster. Now illuminated at night with computer-controlled underwater lighting, the gargoyles appear to breathe fire.

Joseph Paxton designed water temples and cascades for the fountains at Sydenham, London, in 1854. Plumes and skirts of water and networks of fine jets around basins illustrate that from this time fountains were impressive for their use of water alone. Altogether over eleven thousand jets were in play.

In 1854 the Crystal Palace was relocated to Penge Place in Sydenham, south London, where massed water displays were made possible by the invention of specialised water pumps. Two huge fountains installed either side of the main avenue rose 250 feet (76 metres) and dominated the 200 acre (81 hectare) park. By the 1800s ram pumps could lift water to a great height by using the energy of a plentiful supply of falling water such as a stream.

In 1853 W. A. Nesfield designed the *Perseus and Andromeda* fountain at Witley Court in Worcestershire for the first Earl of Dudley, the coal and iron magnate. Easton & Company undertook the engineering for this fountain. Water was pumped from below the Hundred Pool by a 40 horsepower steam engine to a reservoir above the Court. However, pumped water alone was not sufficient to drive the immense fountain and additional sources were

When the Great Court at Athelhampton, Dorset, was laid out in the 1890s the garden-houses on the terrace had water tanks in their pyramidal roofs, feeding four fountains. They worked on a gravity system, with water from the River Piddle pumped by a hydraulic ram up to the reservoirs. They now have electric pumps.

used. Underground pipes carried supplementary water from a dammed stream to the reservoir, which took two and a half days to fill. Water was also taken from the lower Washing Pool. Water pressure for the jets came from gravity feed through the 18 inch (457 mm) diameter down-pipes to the 6 inch (152 mm) diameter up-pipes – the ratio stipulated by Pliny the Elder. Carved in Portland stone, the figures of Perseus and Andromeda are surrounded by water-spraying dolphins and two separate nereids on dolphins placed within the pool.

Nesfield and Easton & Company also re-worked the gardens at Holkham Hall in Norfolk, installing the *St George and Dragon* fountain carved by C. R. Smith in 1856. A steam pump raised well water to fill reservoirs for a gravity feed similar to that at Witley Court. An artesian well was bored in 1867 so that trapped water resting above an impervious layer of rock could be accessed from ground level. Electric pumps still force water through the original lead and cast-iron pipes. Early reservoirs were lined with puddled clay – that is, clay that was trampled down to form a solid base with sloping sides. In the early twentieth century reservoirs of cast iron were replaced by steel.

Patrons with inherited wealth often embellished their properties with sculptural fountains in traditional materials. The seventh Earl of Carlisle acquired the Great Exhibition's *Atlas* fountain carved in Portland stone by John Thomas (see front cover). It was installed in 1853 as the centre of a parterre designed by W. A. Nesfield for Castle Howard in North Yorkshire. Hand-sculpted stone fountains such as these were expensive – the *Perseus and Andromeda* fountain at Witley Court cost £20,000 in the 1850s – which meant that only the immensely wealthy could commission them.

Other costly fountains included two at Waddesdon Manor in Buckinghamshire, where in 1883 Baron Ferdinand de Rothschild installed a marble *Pluto and Proserpine* fountain (by Giuliano Mozani before 1727) on the parterre. At Cliveden in Buckinghamshire the gardens were

The dramatic 'Perseus and Andromeda' fountain at Witley Court, Worcestershire, with a central plume of water over 100 feet (30 metres) high, was described as the largest fountain structure in Europe. Since restoration, the fountain takes twenty minutes to recycle the 2000 gallons (7570 litres) of water for a display lasting twelve minutes. Ten computer-controlled electric pumps drive the jets and ultraviolet light cleans the water.

The marble sculpture of Pluto and Proserpine on the south parterre fountain at Waddesdon Manor, Buckinghamshire, with hippocampi and other aquatic figures spraying water around the central figures. Collectors such as Baron Rothschild liked to adorn their properties with traditional fountains of this kind.

redesigned in the late nineteenth century and the imposing *Fountain of Love* by Waldo Story was installed for the collector, William Waldorf Astor, in 1897. In 1896 the marble Borghese Balustrade carved around 1618 for Cardinal Scipione Borghese was added to the garden. Marble has been carved since antiquity but it is a costly and time-consuming task. For the general public and civic authorities alternative materials were needed that were cheaper, easily formed and acceptable.

On the right of the marble 'Fountain of Love' by Waldo Story at Cliveden, Buckinghamshire, the female with outstretched arms welcomes a little cupid, while on the left the ambrosial elixir has entranced the female, who extends her chalice for more.

The 'Triton' fountain at Culzean Castle, South Ayrshire, was constructed in cast concrete sometime between 1856 and 1893. Other properties have similar fountains set in lakes and serving as centrepieces for parterres.

The process of making Roman cement was long forgotten but Joseph Smeaton rediscovered hydraulic cement in 1756 and in 1796 James Parker patented a hydraulic material called 'Parkes Cement' or 'Roman Cement'. An improved version made in 1824 from Portland stone became more widely used. This simulated stone could be cast into moulds for fountain components, such as the *Triton* fountain at Culzean Castle in Ayrshire.

Another material, Coade stone, was invented around 1769 when Eleanor Coade started her ordering service and production of garden ornaments. Coade stone is a clay-based ceramic, of crushed glass, ball clay and water, with

Philip Thomason used his Coade-stone recipe for this modern 'Whale and Mermaid' fountain at Farleigh House, Hampshire, for the Portsmouth family, whose crest incorporates a mermaid. In 1992 the 1$^{1}/_{2}$ ton whale was produced in one piece and took two weeks to fire. Water sprays from the blow-hole.

The Pulhamite fountain built for the Dunorlan Estate in Kent is 15 feet (5 metres) high and has two basins in candelabrum style. The top section was exhibited at the 1862 International Exhibition. The main basin in Pulhamite is decorated with more delicate terracotta, which weathers better. Water was supplied from a lake sited 15 feet (5 metres) above the fountain simply by opening the valve in the water-pipe when needed.

Right: *The terracotta 'Doulton' fountain on Glasgow Green from the great exhibition of 1888 celebrates the reign of Queen Victoria. The sculpture of the queen is surrounded by four water-carriers and representations of the Empire, the Armed Services and Culture. Possibly the world's largest terracotta fountain, it is 50 feet (15 metres) high and 70 feet (21 metres) in diameter. Terracotta is natural clay that is modelled and dried. It is a material that has been produced since antiquity.*

the clay already pre-fired to prevent shrinkage during manufacture. After being formed in the mould, the piece is finely worked by hand and then dried. Following this, it is fired for several days at a high temperature so that it is frost-proof and durable.

Pulhamite, the trade name for a material coarser than terracotta, was first manufactured in the mid 1840s. It was the invention of James Pulham and although the material was mainly used to replicate natural stonework for cascades it was also much sought after as a material for finer artworks. The exact ingredients are not known. A Pulhamite copy of the fountain of *Florence* at the Villa Medici, Castello, was commissioned for the Dunorlan Estate after 1867, although the Venus figure at the apex was replaced by one of Hebe. The fountain still stands in the public park. By the 1850s terracotta, a buff-coloured earthenware of fine clay, was used for the mass-production of fountains and garden ornaments.

Further developments in the production of simulated stone have provided cost-effective and high-quality products that include fountains.

Since 1885 there have been public gardens near the church of St John the Evangelist in Horseferry Road, London SW1, where this fountain is a memorial. It is in Haddonstone, a modern equivalent of the earlier artificial stone used for mass production of fountains, and, like them, it is available from a catalogue. On this cyclix fountain three dolphins on tail-ends spray water above a lotus basin.

A modern manufacturer, Haddonstone, offers replica Portland stone, Bath stone and terracotta. The production process starts with a model of the piece in plaster or wood, from which a rubber mould is prepared. A dry mix of crushed stone and binder is packed into the mould, which is later removed, and the item cured overnight in a vapour chamber.

Both modern and traditional metals were used for the *Shaftesbury Memorial* fountain in Piccadilly Circus, London, known to many as 'Eros', but intended to represent the Angel of Christian Charity. The aluminium used for the figure has several advantages for fountain decoration; it is malleable, light and resists

On the 'Shaftesbury Memorial' fountain in Piccadilly Circus, London, the nudity of Eros was deemed to be scandalous by contemporary viewers and the putti decoration unsightly. Alfred Gilbert's sculpture of 1893 commemorates the philanthropic works of the seventh Earl of Shaftesbury.

When the Promenade in Cheltenham, Gloucestershire, was improved in 1893, Portland stone (from Portland Bill in Dorset) was used for the new 'Neptune' fountain. Designed by the borough surveyor, Joseph Hall, it was reported in the local press to be both 'very beautiful' and 'the ugliest fountain in Europe'.

corrosion. Sculptures in aluminium were novel in the nineteenth century and this one seems at odds with the massive stem and basins in bronze, carved with classical decoration. The ability to recycle water by electric pumps towards the end of the nineteenth century meant that fountains such as this could be sited away from their original water source. At the beginning of the twentieth century fountain water tanks were of cast iron and pipes of lead had brass end-pieces soldered together, although between 1860 and 1910 the Doulton Company, the leading manufacturer of industrial ceramics, also produced drainpipes made from stone clay.

Sculptures of nymphs and putti carved in Greek marble in the antique manner on the 'Loggia' fountain at Hever Castle, Kent, by William Frith, 1908. The 'Trevi' fountain in Rome inspired both this fountain and the 'Neptune' fountain in Cheltenham, with the inclusion of a massive shell as a focal point.

The twentieth century and beyond

Changes in social conditions, urban regeneration and new technology influenced fountain design during the twentieth century, leading to even more ingenious displays. Private estates and trust foundations commissioned both traditional and contemporary fountain designs to entice visitors to historic sites. At Hever Castle, Kent, and Blenheim Palace, Oxfordshire, traditional designs and water parterres were considered more in keeping with the style of the architecture. The long-lost seventeenth-century gardens by Salomon de Caus at Wilton House in Wiltshire were supplemented in 1969 by David Vickary's fountain for the north forecourt and in 2000 by two large Portland stone fountains by William Pye on the east façade.

Similarly, the owners of properties such as Antony House, Cornwall, and Harewood House, West Yorkshire, have added the work of contemporary artists to their grounds so that traditional and modern water features stand together. A Mughal garden by Harold Peto was installed for the first Lord Faringdon at Buscot Park in Oxfordshire from

In the 1920s Achille Duchêne planned the upper water parterre at Blenheim Palace, Oxfordshire, in the French formal style with geometric pools and fountain jets. The lower parterre has Bernini's scale model of the fountain of the 'Four Rivers' in Rome (1648 to 1651), which had been hidden behind the cascade since 1710.

The memorial fountain at Wilton, Wiltshire, to the sixteenth Earl of Pembroke has three submersible pumps under the driveway, each linked to separate compartments of a header box (a container feeding the water nozzles). It combines fan sprays and nozzles facing upwards and outwards to display a dome of water.

The 'Scala Aquae Pembrochiana' in Portland stone by William Pye at Wilton House supports a series of eight bronze spouts from which water curves down into stepped receiving basins.

Below left: *The Carew family of Antony House in Cornwall added this bronze cone by William Pye in 1996 to the formal topiary garden, replicating the shape of the yew tree beyond. The tactile bronze surface invites children to feel the flow of water down its surface.*

Below right: *At Harewood House, West Yorkshire, the 'Orpheus' (son of a river god) sculpture of 1984 by Astrid Zydower stands on a plinth of black marble shrouded by a film of moving water. The water suggests the hidden depths of the mythological underworld, from which Orpheus returns. The parterre also has two original 'Triton' fountains.*

The intertwined figures of the bronze 'Dolphin and Nymph' fountain at Buscot Park, Oxfordshire, mark the beginning of the water rills and chutes through the woodland course down to the lake.

1904 to 1913 alongside traditional bronze fountains. Modern commissions at Hever Castle and Scone Palace near Perth have water mazes that follow a watery path or lead the visitors to a spectacular fountain.

New materials and modern technology have replaced the sculptural details and mythological associations of traditional fountains. For example, the visitor's attention is held when the force of water moves two fountains by Angela Conner, the *Revelation* fountain at Chatsworth House and *Rolling Stones* in Dublin, Ireland. A variation of spinning stones in which the Kugel stone turns in a granite socket is to be found at Carsington Water, Derbyshire.

Above: 'Giochi d'aqua' or trick fountains may soak participants in the Water Maze at Hever Castle, Kent, designed by Adrian Fisher and installed in 1997. Stone slabs set above water tilt when stood on, triggering water jets from between the paving. In 'Hypnerotomachia Poliphili' (1499) Poliphilo experienced a similar trick after placing his foot on a step to activate a spray in his face.

Right: Water jets spray the bronze 'Arethusa' figure by David Williams Ellis (1990) at the centre of the Murray Star Maze at Scone Palace near Perth. In mythology the nymph Arethusa raises herself to tell Ceres that she has seen Proserpine in the underworld. She is subsequently transformed into a spring.

Above left: *Resembling a pomegranate, the 'Revelation' fountain at Chatsworth House, from 1999, is driven by surging water as the globe rises and falls within the shell. The globe emerges from within the petals with water gushing from the apex before falling into the clasp of the petals as water surges from its base.*

Above right: *In 1992 the Kugel stone was installed at Carsington Water in Derbyshire. The 3 foot (90 cm) diameter natural granite sphere rotates within a granite socket as water is pumped into the socket at two different speeds, allowing the stone to spin in suspension.*

'Rolling Stones' at West Park, Dublin, by Angela Conner comprises two spheres, one of white marble dust and resin and the other of slate dust and resin, each measuring 6 feet (1.8 metres) in diameter. The weight of the water collected inside the stones causes them to roll and, while doing so, to discharge water.

The water display at Alnwick Castle in Northumberland has pools, rills, cascades and water walls fed from the main water supply. Water is recycled at a rate of 66 gallons (300 litres) a second for the cascade and 128 gallons (580 litres) for the fountains. Rills and chutes (low-stepped cascades) feature throughout the gardens. Opened in 2002, the water garden was based on a design for the Hofgarten at Wurzburg, Germany, taken from an unused plan of 1774.

Sustained, sequential and automated displays are controlled by computers sited near such fountains as that at Kiftsgate Court in Gloucestershire, which has a choreographed water display (see page 3). In addition, monitors can regulate the speed of electric water pumps and control the flow and levels of water to ensure an optimum performance. Unique in size and scale, the water gardens at Alnwick Castle in Northumberland have computers controlling 150 nozzles independently in any combination. The central cascade has twenty-seven weirs, with water disappearing through four bell-mouthed openings before reappearing as four mounds of water. Simultaneously, 120 jumping jets shoot water over the walkway to the grand basin beyond. Jumping jets have fast-acting valves driven by the build-up of pressure in air cylinders to produce a sudden burst jet. Water maintenance is provided by trawler nets to filter water that is recycled with added chemicals (which are both human and animal friendly).

In 1992 Richard Chaix designed one of the first water features controlled by computer technology, for Cabot Square in Canary Wharf, London. In cities bubble-jet fountains produce varying displays of water recycled into their receiving basins, as in Cabot Square, or simply as washdown fountains, as in Russell Square, London. Courtyards at Somerset House and Burlington House in London also have washdown displays – examples of the new interactive generation of fountains that allow children to play between the jets in summer.

In 1992 this circular black granite basin with intersecting lines of frothy bubble-jets was installed in Cabot Square, Canary Wharf, London. An anemometer in the trees nearby adjusts the jets to prevent drifting spray. The feature is set above the road level with surrounding stepped cascades of water on each side of the square.

Above: *A similar effect to that of the Cabot Square installation is achieved in the Botanic Gardens in Cambridge, where the fountain by David Mellor (1970) has jets rising above the water from raised bronze discs. The water in the pool surrounding the disc fountains is disturbed but a metal band separates this from the outer pool, which remains calm in contrast.*

Right: *Plumes of water rise and fall from 20 feet (6 metres) in Russell Square, the largest square in London. This is a washdown fountain, where water drains through grilles or crevices before being recycled, offering an interactive feature for public enjoyment and limiting the opportunity for vandalism to the material or water supply of the fountain.*

Below: *Multi-use of city space means that washdown fountains enable a 'fountain area' to be used as a paved space for exhibitions and events when the fountains are not in use. Theatrical fibre-optic lighting and the varying computer-controlled fountain heights give an extra dimension to the Edmund J. Safra Court at Somerset House, London, during the evenings.*

In 1845 water for the red granite fountains in Trafalgar Square was originally supplied from artesian wells in front of and behind the National Gallery, where the engine-room raising the water was also sited. By 1948 the two fountains had been redesigned to commemorate two admirals from the First World War, Lord Jellicoe and Lord Beatty.

Right: *The Barbican Centre's water chute flows into a large rectangular lake flanked with circular bubble-jet fountains. These and the general waterscape were originally provided as part of the cooling system for the centre's air-conditioning, particularly that of the concert hall. The chute originally recycled and aerated the lake water.*

Fountains in urban areas reflect the changing use of space and the needs of society. As early as 1948 the fountains in Trafalgar Square, London, originally included to break up the paved area, were enlivened by additional sculptures of mermaids and mermen. Water features were

used extensively at the Barbican Centre in the City of London from 1962 to 1982 to link housing, entertainment facilities and schools. The regeneration of the Docklands and business areas in London has produced relaxing spaces for city workers such as Thames Barrier Park, Broadgate and Jubilee Place, with smooth cascades or turbulent spouts and streams. The works of William Pye, the foremost modern fountain designer in Britain, improve many locations, both private and public; for example, in London the *Chalice* and *Argosy* fountains combine traditional and contemporary materials with titles from antiquity.

A view of the Water Plaza looking towards Green Dock at the Thames Barrier Park, London. The water jets introduce the visitor to the park while masking the road noise. Silver and grey granite paving has four rows of water jets of variable heights, and stainless-steel bollards appear as solid water forms.

Five shallow steps lead down to an oblong pool scattered with granite blocks and slate discs in this shallow cascade in Exchange Square, Broadgate, London, by Skidmore, Owings and Merrill (1991). The intention is not to mask conversations, as in antiquity, but to invite the lunchtime crowds to sit and relax beside the frothing cascade.

Right: Jubilee Place, beside the underground station in Canary Wharf, is enlivened by a long series of raised cascades over shallow steps with rocks and plume jets producing a white-water effect. The dry-stone walling and the rough water suggest a natural stream.

The green bronze 'Sibirica' fountain by William Pye in the Iris Garden, Holland Park, London (1999), projects water in a laminar flow (a smooth water flow in which parallel layers of water have different relative speeds) into four deflecting basins that produce fan-shaped sprays in the pool. 'Sibirica' is the name of the blue and purple Siberian irises that surround the fountain.

In 1991 the stainless-steel bowl of the 'Chalice' fountain, measuring 20 feet (6 metres) in diameter, was suspended 10 feet (3 metres) above the ground in the Colonnades shopping arcade on Buckingham Palace Road, London. Water from jets within the fountain emerges through the base of the bowl to flow over a bronze cone.

Right: Associations with shipping at the Lloyd's Register in Fenchurch Street, London, were reinforced by William Pye's stainless-steel 'Argosy' fountain in 1997. Water slides over the sides of the hull-shaped sculpture and clings to its underside in an effect known as 'coanda'.

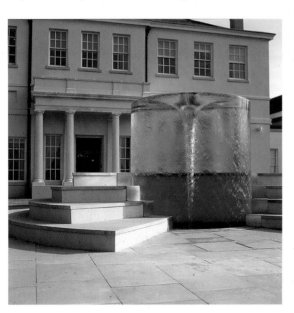

The 'Charybdis' water feature by William Pye at Seaham Hall, County Durham (2000). This acrylic tank holds water entering under high pressure and exceeding the natural drain. An air-core vortex is formed as water is rotated from two points at the base while an inverter slows the speed at the top. A roll wave of water slides over the sides to suggest a solid mass of uncontained water. The reservoir is below the cylinder.

The 'Libra' water sculpture in brushed steel by Angela Conner, at Atlantic House, London EC1, works on the principal of water tipping alternately into two vessels, the tipping being caused by the alternating weight of the water. The sculpture is 94 feet (29 metres) high. In 1206 Al Jazarì had invented a wall fountain called an alternating or tipping fountain that worked on the same principal. It had two vessels filling alternately with water, each of which, on overflowing, would tilt and nudge the inlet pipe to fill the other vessel.

In 1914 stainless steel was invented in Sheffield – a hard metal that even when exposed to weather is protected from corrosion by a film of chromium oxide. This steel may be finished by brushing, hammering and polishing to a high sheen in order to display water in a variety of effects. Water appearing as thin wires fascinates viewers of the steel *Revolving Torsion* fountain by Naum Gabo, and water seemingly sliding in slow motion down polished steel water walls by Alan Wilson is mesmerising. The colour and patina of copper add to the aesthetic appeal of some fountains, such as the unique fountain at the Royal Brompton Hospital, London, and the much-copied *Dandelion* fountain designed in 1960 for the El Alamein Memorial in Sydney, Australia.

City-centre refurbishment often combines the work of earlier and contemporary artists with advanced technology. Fibre optics and LEDs (light-emitting diodes) can produce night-time illumination for

The stainless-steel 'Revolving Torsion' fountain (1973) in the grounds of St Thomas' Hospital, London, has 1500 jets of water and is rotated by an electric motor with a pressure sensor activating a reverse-flow of water to remove pondweed.

Alan Wilson's stainless-steel water wall 'Wave', situated outside the Marriott Hotel in Kensington, London, is a narrow weir that fills with water and gently overflows. Gravity and surface tension affect the flow so that a clear band of water appears at the top and gradually breaks up lower down. On a microscopic level some of the water is not moving at all; the surface tension adheres water to the surface so that water rolls over water.

Right: *The 'Dandelion' fountain, first designed in 1960, has been emulated worldwide. Seen here as the 'Millennium' fountain at Nuneaton, Warwickshire, the head of bronze and copper jets on a stainless-steel stem has a water supply recycled from a pool below with an internal pump and filter.*

Below: *At the Royal Brompton Hospital in London a fountain was designed by Dr Philip Kilner to represent the human heart. Water pulses through lobes similar in shape to those of the heart.*

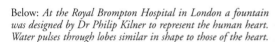

Barry Mason's stainless-steel 'Thales' fountain in the Savill Garden of Windsor Great Park (2002) has a recycling system that seemingly spins water from annuli. Thales, an ancient Greek philosopher, considered that everything originated from and returned to water.

Right: *The sides of the rill at Columbus Courtyard, Canary Wharf, London, have LEDs within a transparent holder, allowing dots of light to appear at intervals along the sides. The casing of the LED incorporates algicides, fungicides and chlorine inhibitors to guarantee optimum performance at all times.*

The light effects at Columbus Courtyard are by Crescent Lighting. Fibre-optic cables are held by small stainless-steel fittings mounted in adjustable clamps to the fountain-head so that light travels along the jet of water. They are aligned with the water flow, with one power point remotely controlling all outlets.

Six hundred years of metal craftsmanship and precision engineering are celebrated in the 1998 Peace Gardens, Sheffield. The theme of water, metalwork and stone is illustrated by the use of millstone grit, the stone used in the industry. Giant bronze vessels on carved stone plinths gush water into weirs and then onwards to eighty-nine computer-controlled jets in the centre of the garden.

fountains. These are seen at Columbus Courtyard, Canary Wharf, where computer programs adjust and control the display of light and colour within the water. Fibre-optic lighting in the fountains tints the jets in the Peace Gardens of Sheffield with the predominant colour of silvery-gold, alluding to metal smelting. Other illuminated water features can be seen in the water plaza in Piccadilly Gardens, Manchester, constructed in 2002, where a viewing footpath crosses above 180 computer-controlled jets.

Redevelopment of cities usually includes the addition and replanning of water features – for example the installation of fountains in Centenary and Exchange Squares in Birmingham and the removal of the road and its replacement with a pedestrian area around the *Queen Victoria Memorial* fountain in The Mall, London. These and other fountains

Jets of changing colour appear within the water display in Piccadilly Gardens, Manchester. Four larger aerated jets rise to 20 feet (6 metres) during the display and are visible from a raised viewing platform. In the summer months they are made accessible for children to play among the sprays.

Industry, enterprise and commerce are celebrated in the 'Spirit of Enterprise' fountain in Centenary Square, Birmingham, by Tom Lomax (1991). A misty spray surrounds the head appearing from a coin above a vice as the water recycles in a representation of commerce returning wealth to the world.

improve what would otherwise be less attractive and accessible urban spaces. Fountains may provide charity collection points, celebrate life and remembrance, and commemorate recent events. One site that illustrates national interest in garden history is the Botanic Gardens in Carmarthenshire, Wales. Visitors follow watercourses and pass fountains

Below left: *Dhruva Mistry's bronze sculpture of 'The River' (1990–3) in Victoria Square, Birmingham, bears an uncanny resemblance to Picasso's 'La Source'. A quotation from T. S. Eliot's 'Four Seasons' engraved on the basin begins with 'And the pool was filled with water out of sunlight'. A lower pool has two youthful figures surrounded by geometric shapes.*

Below right: *The 82 foot (25 metre) high 'Queen Victoria Memorial' fountain designed by Aston Webb and completed in 1924 now stands in a traffic-free zone in The Mall, London. Built of Carrara marble and granite, the fountain has six bronze groups and a statue of Queen Victoria. 108 gallons (491 litres) of water an hour come from the pumping station of the lake in St James's Park before returning to the lake.*

Fountains may be used to disguise unsightly features in urban areas, as seen here at the corner of Concert Hall Approach and Belvedere Road opposite the Royal Festival Hall in London. This fountain has a central jet and curving arcs of water to conceal the domed roof of the car park below, giving the impression of a small city park.

Right: *Money collected in the 'Horses of Helios' fountain by Rudy Weller on the corner of Haymarket in London is for the Disabled Living Foundation. Constructed in 1992, four bronze horses rear in a black marble basin in front of water cascades.*

The circular 'Fountain of Joy' in Hyde Park, London, dates from 1963 but was redesigned in 2001. Bronze sculptures by T. B. Huxley Jones show a dancing couple among bubble-jets and sprays with four children leaping and diving into the water from stones of different colours. Water overflows from eight lips into the surrounding pool.

Slow-moving water glides down these angled stone ramps by Pierre Granache (1994) in Green Park, London. Emblematic of Canada, sculpted maple leaves decorate the surfaces of the memorial to Canadian soldiers who died in the Second World War, and leaves fall from the trees above.

Right: *The Festival Garden fountains in Battersea, London, dating from 1951, were replaced in 2003 by water-walls in the shape of the Crystal Palace, mushroom fountains and arching jets. Any pressure beyond a certain point in water-walls such as this makes the plume of water break into droplets, but monitors control the display.*

The Botanic Gardens of Wales in Carmarthenshire, opened in 2000, display contemporary fountain designs including this water rill over black and white cobbles leading to the 'Circle of Decision'. This is reminiscent of the choice of pathways for Good or Evil that lead through the Villa d'Este at Tivoli from the 1570s.

Local amenities are continually updated with water features, such as Lister Park in Bradford, where a Mughal garden has cascades, chutes and pools. Such gardens were typical in India between the sixteenth and the nineteenth century. The relationship between architecture and garden is a feature of the Mughal style and has been emphasised here by the sandstone used for the Cartwright Hall Art Gallery and the hard landscaping of the garden.

before being offered a choice of direction through the gardens. At Lister Park in Bradford the garden modelled on Mughal water features recognises the importance of earlier styles yet links them with modern needs.

A memorial fountain to Diana, Princess of Wales, designed by Kathryn Gustafson, was opened in Hyde Park, London, in July 2004. The oval rill in Cornish granite is the size of a football pitch and incorporates a changing pattern of water flow from torrents to reflecting pools. Innovative fountains and water features such as this have proved to be of enduring appeal and will no doubt continue to evolve, surprise, delight and impress for many years to come.

In July 2004 the Diana Princess of Wales Memorial Fountain was inaugurated in Hyde Park, London. Water from the Serpentine is channelled around either side of the feature. On the eastern side water is pumped to form cascades down to stepping stones and a languid pool. On the west a gentle flow becomes a waterfall until both waters meet.

Further information

BOOKS

Cooper, Guy, *et al. English Water Gardens*. Weidenfeld & Nicolson, 1996.

Hopwood, Rosalind. *The Origins of the Renaissance Figure Fountain*. PhD thesis, number DX 216265, 2 volumes. The British Library Thesis Department and The British Library Document Supply Centre.

Hudson, Norman. *Hudson's Historic Houses and Gardens*. Norman Hudson & Company, published annually.

Jellicoe, G. and S. *The Use of Water in Landscape Architecture*. Adam & Charles Black, 1971.

Jellicoe, G. and S. *Oxford Companion to Gardens*. Oxford University Press, second edition 2001.

Plumptre, George. *The Water Garden*. Thames & Hudson, 2003.

Ridgeway, Christopher (editor). *William Andrews Nesfield*. University of York, 1996.

Symmes, Marilyn (editor). *Fountains, Splash and Spectacle*. Thames & Hudson, 1998.

WEBSITES

English Heritage: www.engheritage.org.uk

The Fountain Society: www.fountainsoc.org.uk

Historic Houses Association: www.hha.org.uk

The National Trust: www.nationaltrust.org.uk

The National Trust for Scotland: www.nts.org.uk

THE FOUNTAIN SOCIETY

The Fountain Society promotes the preservation of fountains and their provision in new developments for public enjoyment. Details of membership, activities and fountains listed by the society are available from the website (see above) or by post (The Fountain Society, 26 Binney Street, London W1K 5BL).

The fountain in the small cloister of Westminster Abbey (1871) is the inspiration for the logo of the Fountain Society.

Fountains and water features to visit

The fountains and water features listed here are open to the public at certain times of the year but intending visitors are advised to check the opening times, performance of the fountains and access in advance. It has been possible to include only a selection of London's fountains.

ABBREVIATIONS

EH	English Heritage	NTS	National Trust for Scotland
HHA	Historic Houses Association	NW	Fountain not working
HS	Historic Scotland	PO	Privately owned
LA	Local authority	SO	State-owned (Italy)
NT	National Trust		

ENGLAND
Bedfordshire
Wrest Park Gardens (EH), Silsoe MK45 4HS. Telephone: 01525 860152. ('Long Water', rectangular pools, bath-house.)

Berkshire
Legoland, Winkfield Road, Windsor SL4 4AY. Telephone: 08705 040404. Website: www.lego.com/legoland (Cascade over the maze designed by Adrian Fisher, 1996.)
Savill Garden (Crown Estate), Windsor Great Park SL4 2HT. Telephone: 01753 847518. Website: www.savillgarden.co.uk ('Thales' fountain by Barry Mason [www.sculpture.org.uk], stones and bubble-jet fountain in the Temperate House dedicated to Queen Elizabeth the Queen Mother, 1995.)
Virginia Water Lake, Windsor Great Park, near the A30/A329 junction. Website: www.thecrownestate.co.uk (Cascade.)

Buckinghamshire
Cliveden (NT), Taplow, Maidenhead SL6 0JA. Telephone: 01494 755562 (infoline) or 01628 605069. (The 'Fountain of Love', 'The Tortoise' fountain [NW] and the Borghese Balustrade.)
Stowe Gardens and Park (NT), near Buckingham MK18 5EH. Telephone: 01296 653211 (infoline) or 01280 822850. (Cascade between the Eleven-Acre Lake and the Octagonal Lake. 'The Four Seasons' fountain made from a fireplace in 1702.)
Waddesdon Manor (NT), near Aylesbury HP18 0JH. Telephone: 01296 653211 (infoline) or 01296 653203. Website: www.waddesdon.org.uk ('Pluto and Proserpine' and 'Triton and Nereid' fountains.)
West Wycombe Park (NT), West Wycombe HP14 3AJ. Telephone: 01494 513569. (Cascade with sculpted nymphs.)

Cambridgeshire
Cambridge University Botanic Garden, Cory Lodge, Bateman Street, Cambridge CB2 1JF. Website: www.botanic.cam.ac.uk (Fountain on the Main Walk, 1970.)
Department of Engineering, Cambridge University, Trumpington Street, Cambridge CB2 1PZ. Telephone: 01223 332600. Website: www.eng.cam.ac.uk (Patinated bronze 'Blades' fountain by David Mellor, 1987.)
Gonville and Caius College, Trinity Street, Cambridge CB2 1TA. Website: www.cai.cam.ac.uk (Monument fountain by H. A. Armistead, 1879.)

Cheshire
Lady Lever Art Gallery, The Diamond, Port Sunlight, Wirral CH26 5EQ. Telephone: 0151 478 4136. Website: www.liverpoolmuseums.org. ('Sea Spirit' fountain by Charles Wheeler, 1950.)
Lyme Park (NT), Disley, Stockport SK12 2NX. Telephone: 01663 762023. (Former Dutch garden, fountain in the Orangery and 'Prince of Wales' plume fountain.)

Cornwall
Antony House and Garden (NT), Torpoint, Plymouth PL11 2QA. Telephone: 01752 812191. (The 'Cone' fountain by William Pye.)
Mount Edgcumbe House and Country Park (LA), Cremyll, Torpoint PL10 1NF. Telephone: 01752 822236. Website: www.mountedgcumbe.gov.uk ('Mermaid' fountain, *c.*1816, and a geyser in the New Zealand Garden.)

Cumbria
Holker Hall and Gardens (HHA), Cark-in-Cartmel, Grange-over-Sands LA11 7PL. Telephone: 01539 558328. Website: www.holker-hall.co.uk (Limestone cascade and fountain.)

Derbyshire
Bolsover Castle (EH), Castle Street, Bolsover S44 6PR. Telephone: 01246 822844. ('Venus' fountain.)
Chatsworth House (Chatsworth House Trust), Bakewell DE45 1PP. Telephone: 01246 565300. Website: www.chatsworth.org (The Canal Pond, 'Cascade', 'Duck' fountain, 'Emperor' fountain, the 'Grotto of Venus', 'Revelation' fountain, 'Sea-Horse and Triton' fountain and the 'Willow Tree' fountain.)
Derby Cascade, Market Place, Derby. Website: www.williampye.com (Semicircular cascade by William Pye, 1993.)
Melbourne Hall (HHA), Church Square, Melbourne DE73 1EN. Telephone: 01332 862502. Website: www.melbournehall.com (Fountains in the yew walk and woodland gardens.)

Devon
Coleton Fishacre House and Garden (NT), Brownstone Road, Kingswear, Dartmouth TQ6 0EQ. Telephone: 01803 752466. (Cyclix fountain with central jet and rill.)

Dorset
Athelhampton House and Gardens (HHA), Athelhampton, Dorchester DT2 7LG. Telephone: 01305 848363. Website: www.athelhampton.co.uk (Fountains in compartment gardens and canal.)
Mapperton Gardens (HHA), Beaminster DT8 3NR. Telephone: 01308 862645. Website: www.mapperton.com (Shaped 1920s pool and fountain.)

Durham
Seaham Hall, Lord Byron's Walk, Seaham SR7 7AG. Telephone: 0191 516 1400. Website: www.williampye.com ('Charybdis' water feature by William Pye.)

Essex
Braintree: junction of High Street and South Street ('George V Memorial' fountain by John Hodge, 1936); location under consideration (Bronze boy on an upright shell).

Gloucestershire and Bristol
Bristol: Millennium Square, Cannon's Marsh. Website: www.williampye.com ('Aquarena' by William Pye, 2000.)

Cheltenham: The Promenade. ('Neptune' fountain.)
Hidcote Manor Garden (NT), Hidcote Bartrim, Chipping Campden GL55 6LR. Telephone: 01386
   438333. Website: www.nationaltrust.org.uk/hidcote ('Putto' fountain in the Pool Garden.)
Kiftsgate Court Gardens (PO), Hidcote Bartrim, Chipping Campden GL55 6LN. Telephone:
   01386 438777. Website: www.kiftsgate.co.uk (Fountain by Simon Allison, 2001, and the
   'Labours of the Months'.)
Painswick Rococo Garden (HHA), Painswick GL6 6TH. Telephone: 01452 813204. Website:
   www.rococogarden.co.uk (Cold bath and spring.)
Stanway House and Water Garden (HHA), Stanway, Cheltenham GL54 5PQ. Telephone: 01386
   584469. Website: www.stanwayfountain.co.uk (Canal with a jet fountain, plus cascade and
   waterfall under restoration in 2004.)
Westbury Court (NT), Westbury-on-Severn GL14 1PD. Telephone: 01452 760461. (Dutch
   water garden.)

Hampshire
Exbury Gardens (HHA), Exbury, Southampton SO45 1AZ. Telephone: 023 8089 1203.
   Website: www.exbury.co.uk (Natural gardens with several pools and cascades.)
Farleigh House (PO), Farleigh Wallop, near Basingstoke RG25 2HT. Telephone: 01256 842684.
   (Coade-stone 'Whale and Mermaid' fountain [see www.coadestone.com]. Viewings by appointment.)
Queen Eleanor's Garden (LA), The Great Hall, Castle Avenue, Winchester SO23 8UJ.
   Telephone: 01962 846476. Website: www.hants.gov.uk ('Falcon' fountain.)

Herefordshire
Hampton Court (PO), Hope under Dinmore, Leominster HR6 0PN. Telephone: 01568
   797777. Website: www.hamptoncourt.org.uk (Water gardens.)

Hertfordshire
Hatfield House and Gardens (PO), Hatfield AL9 5NQ. Telephone: 01707 287010. www.hatfield-
   house.co.uk (Fountains in the Scented Garden, Privy Garden and Kitchen Garden.)

Isle of Wight
Osborne House (EH), East Cowes PO32 6JY. Telephone: 01983 200022. ('Boy and Swan'
   fountain in bronzed zinc, bronze 'Andromeda' fountain by John Bell bought at the Great
   Exhibition, and 'Kneeling Venus' fountain.)

Kent
Dunorlan Estate, Tunbridge Wells. (Pulhamite fountain [see www.pulham.org.uk])
Hever Castle (HHA), Hever, Edenbridge TN8 7NG. Telephone: 01732 865224. Website:
   www.hevercastle.co.uk ('Loggia' fountain, 'Millennium' fountain and water maze.)
Walmer Castle and Gardens (EH), Walmer, Deal CT14 7LJ. Telephone: 01304 364288.
   (Reflecting pool in the Queen Mother's Garden.)

Lancashire
Beetham Plaza, Drury Lane, Liverpool. ('The Bucket' fountain with pivoting steel cups, 1967,
   restored 2000.)
Manchester: Albert Square. ('Queen Victoria' fountain.)
Manchester: Piccadilly Gardens. (Water plaza with washdown fountains and mist sprays, 2002.)
Miller Park (LA), Preston. Website: www.visitpreston.com (Fountain by C. R. Smith in
   Longridge stone, costing £213 3s 7d in the mid nineteenth century.)
The Urbis Centre, Cathedral Gardens, Manchester. Website: www.urbis.org.uk (Water plaza
   with rill and jet fountains between posts, 2001.)

The seventeen water jets at Burlington House, London, encircle the statue of Sir Joshua Reynolds, mapping out the astronomy of his birth date, 16th July 1723. The composer Handel lived here for five years and the fountains are choreographed by computer to his 'Water Music', using both intervals and musical notes for a four-minute programme of water display every half-hour.

Leicestershire

Leicester Town Hall (LA), Bishop Street, Leicester. (Victorian fountain by Francis Hames, 1897.)
University of Leicester, University Road, Leicester. ('Four Fold' fountain by Stephen Collingbourne, 1997.)

London and Middlesex

Atlantic House, 65 Holborn Viaduct, EC1A 2DY (A–Z: 6K 161). ('Libra' fountain by Angela Conner in the atrium of Lovells [see www.burleighfield.co.uk].)
Barbican (LA), Silk Street, EC2Y 8DS (A–Z: 5D 162). Website: www.barbican.org (Water chute and fountains.)
Battersea Gardens (LA), Battersea, SW11 4NJ. (A–Z: 7E 84). Website: www.wandsworth.gov.uk (Festival water gardens and fountain in the English Garden.)
Belvedere Road and Concert Hall Approach, SE1 (A–Z: 6H 167). (Fountain above the domed roof of the car park.)
Burlington House, 178–80 Piccadilly, W1J 9ER (A–Z: 7G 67). Telephone: 020 7300 8000. (Washdown fountains.)
Bushy Park, Chestnut Avenue, Bushy Park, off Hampton Court Road, near Hampton Court Palace (A–Z: 2K 133). Website: www.royalparks.gov.uk (The 'Diana' fountain.)

John Ravera sculpted the bronze 'Dolphin' fountain unveiled in Ben Jonson Place at the Barbican Centre in 1990. During the sixteenth and seventeenth centuries many literary figures lived in this area.

Cabot Square, Canary Wharf, E14 (A–Z: 1C 88). (Bubble fountain pool and surrounding cascades.)

Cannizaro Park, Wimbledon, SW19 (A–Z: 6E 118). Website: www.watermarkhydro.com (Bronze multi-spouted 'Urn' fountain by Richard Rome, 2001.)

Chiswick House (EH), Burlington Lane, W4 2RP (A–Z: 6A 82). Telephone: 020 8995 0508. (Two-tier cascade, 1738.)

Colonnades Shopping Centre, Buckingham Palace Road, Victoria, SW1 (A–Z: 4F 85). Website: www.williampye.com ('Chalice' fountain by William Pye.)

Cottons Landing, Preston's Road, Isle of Dogs, E14 (A–Z: 2E 88). ('Leap' fountain by Franta Belsky, 1987.)

Cutler's Gardens, Houndsditch, EC3 (A–Z: 7H 163). (Architectural water features with cascades, 1982.)

Dolphin Square, Westminster, SW1 (A–Z: 6B 172). ('Dolphin' fountain by James Butler, 1987.)

Edmund J. Safra Fountain Court (Somerset House Trust), Somerset House, Strand, WC2R 1LA (A–Z: 2G 167). Telephone: 020 7845 4600. Website: www.somerset-house.org.uk (Washdown fountains.)

Exchange Square, Broadgate, EC2 (A–Z: 5G 163). Website: www.broadgatelondon.com (Cascades and watercourse.)

Festival Gardens, St Paul's Cathedral, Cannon Street, EC4 (A–Z: 1C 168). (Lion-mask wall fountains.)

Fountains Court, Middle Temple, EC4 (A–Z: 1J 167). (Memorial fountain, 1976.)

Fulham Palace and Museum (London Borough of Hammersmith and Fulham and Fulham Palace Trust), Bishop's Avenue, Fulham, SW6 6EA (A–Z: 2G 101). Telephone: 020 7736 3233. (Courtyard fountain.)

Green Park, SW1 (A–Z: 6K 165). ('Canadian War Memorial' water feature.)

Guildhall Piazza, Nun Court, EC2 (A–Z: 6E 162). (Glass-mosaic fountain by Allen David, 1969.)

Hampton Court Palace (Historic Royal Palaces), KT8 9AU (A–Z: 4A 133). Telephone: 020 8781 9500. Website: www.hrp.org.uk (The Long Water, 'Queen Elizabeth II Jubilee' fountain, a wall fountain, and fountains in the Privy Garden, Fountain Courtyard and Parterre.)

Haymarket, corner of Piccadilly Circus, SW1 (A–Z: 3C 166). ('Horses of Helios' charity fountain.)

Hay's Galleria, Tooley Street, SE1 (A–Z: 4G 169). Website: www.haysgalleria.co.uk (Bronze 'Navigators' charity fountain by David Kemp, 1987.)

Holland Park, Kensington, W8 (A–Z: 2H 83). Website: www.williampye.com ('Sibirica' fountain by William Pye.)

Hyde Park, off Park Lane, W1 (A–Z: 4G 165). Website: www.royalparks.gov.uk ('Joy of Life' fountain, formerly the 'Four Winds' fountain of 1963, redesigned in 2001; marble 'Boy and Dolphin' fountain in the Rose Garden, 1862; 'Diana' fountain, by Feodora Gleichen, 1906, in the Rose Garden, towards the east end of Rotten Row; Princess Diana Memorial Fountain, 2004.)

Inner Temple Gardens, Embankment, EC4 (A–Z: 2K 167). ('Dolphin' fountain.)

Jubilee Place, Canary Wharf, West India Docks, E14 (A–Z: 1D 88). Website: www.canarywharf.com (Long rustic cascades with bubble jets.)

Kensington Gardens, near Inverness Terrace Gate, Diana Memorial Playground, W2 (A–Z: 1A 84). Website: www.royalparks.gov.uk (Water features and 'Mermaid' fountain.)

Kensington Gardens, near Marlborough Gate, The Italian Gardens, W2 (A–Z: 3A 164). Website: www.royalparks.gov.uk (Formal water parterre and cascade.)

KPMG Courtyard, Dorset Rise, EC4 (A–Z: 1A 168). ('St George and Dragon' fountain by Michael Sandler, 1988.)

Lloyd's Register, Fenchurch Street, EC3 (A–Z: 1G 169). ('Argosy' fountain by William Pye.)

The Mall, SW1 (A–Z: 7A 166). ('Queen Victoria Memorial' fountain.)

Marriott Hotel, 147 Cromwell Road, Kensington, SW5 0TH (A–Z: 4B 84). ('Wave' water feature [see www.thesculptureworkshop.co.uk].)

New Palace Gardens, Westminster, Parliament Square, SW1 (A–Z: 7E 166). ('Silver Jubilee' fountain by Valenty Patel, 1977.)

Piccadilly Circus, W1 (LA) (A–Z: 3C 166). ('Shaftesbury Memorial' fountain.)

Royal Brompton Hospital, Sydney Street, SW3 (A–Z: 5H 69). (Copper 'Heart' fountain.)

Royal Exchange Buildings (NW), Cornhill, EC3 (A–Z: 1F 169). (Drinking fountain with bronze figure.)

Russell Square (LA), Bloomsbury, WC1 (A–Z: 4E 160). (Washdown fountain.)

St Bartholomew's Hospital (NW), West Smithfield Road, EC1 (A–Z: 6B 162). (Terracotta fountain by Philip Hardwick, 1859, restored 1990.)

St Christopher's Place, Marylebone, W1 (A–Z: 7H 159). Website: www.williampye.com ('Cristos' fountain by William Pye, 1993.)

St John the Evangelist, Horseferry Road, Westminster, SW1 (A–Z: 2D 172). (Haddonstone 'Dolphin' fountain [see www.haddonstone.co.uk].)

St Katharine's Dock, E1 (A–Z: 3K 169). ('Girl with a Dolphin' fountain by David Wynne, 1973.)

St Paul's Churchyard, Covent Garden, WC2 (A–Z: 2F 167). (Coade-stone river-god mask fountain by Philip Thomason, 1997 [see www.coadestone.com].)

St Thomas' Hospital, Lambeth Palace Road, SE1 7EH (A–Z: 7G 167). Telephone: 020 7928 9292. ('Revolving Torsion' fountain, on loan from the Tate Gallery.)

Sloane Square, Belgravia, SW1 (A–Z: 4F 171). ('Kneeling Venus' fountain by Gilbert Ledward, 1953.)

Surrey Quays Shopping Centre, SE16 (A–Z: 3J 87). ('Dolphin' fountain by David Backhouse.)

Syon House, Syon Park, Brentford TW8 8JF (A–Z: 1C 98). Telephone: 020 8560 0882. Website: www.syonpark.co.uk (Bronze 'Mercury' fountain, after Giambologna.)

Thames Barrier Park (LA), Barrier Point Road, E16 2HP (A–Z: 2A 90). Website: www.thamesbarrierpark.org.uk (Water plaza.)

Tower Bridge Piazza, Horseleydown Lane, Bermondsey, SE1 (A–Z: 6J 169). (Bronze figures and waterfall around a concrete basin by Anthony Donaldson, 1991.)

Trafalgar Square (LA), Westminster, WC2 (A–Z: 4D 166). (Two fountains.)

Victoria and Albert Museum, South Kensington, SW7 2RL (A–Z: 2B 170). Telephone: 020 7942 2000. (Small bronze figure fountain dating from *c*.1430s, marble Neptune and Triton figures by Bernini, 1622 for Cardinal Montalto in Rome, and marble basin by Pietro Tacca, 1620 from Florence.)

West Smithfield Gardens, EC1 (A–Z: 6A 162). ('Peace' fountain and bronze figure fountain.)

Westminster Abbey, Dean's Yard, Westminster, SW1P 3NP (A–Z: 1E 172). Website: www.westminster-abbey.org.uk (Little Cloister fountain.)

York House, Twickenham (A–Z: 1B 116). (Cascade with statuary, 1911.)

Norfolk

Blickling Hall (NT), Blickling, Norwich NR11 6NF. Telephone: 01263 738030. (Fountain in the formal garden.)

Holkham Hall (HHA), Wells-next-the-Sea NR23 1AB. Telephone: 01328 710227. Website: www.holkham.co.uk ('St George and Dragon' fountain, 1856.)

Northumberland

Alnwick Castle (HHA), Alnwick NE66 1NQ. Telephone: 01665 511100. Website: www.alnwickgarden.com (Water garden, cascade, rills and pools.)

Chillingham Castle (HHA), near Alnwick NE66 5NJ. Telephone: 01668 215359. Website: www.chillingham-castle.com (Fountain on the parterre.)

This bronze 'Mermaid' fountain in the Italian garden at Blenheim Palace was commissioned from Waldo Story in 1908. Water from the fountain overflows into the tambourines of the supporting nymphs, replicating the rhythmic pattering sound of the instrument.

Oxfordshire

Blenheim Palace (HHA), Woodstock OX20 1PX. Telephone: 08700 602080. Website: www.blenheimpalace.com ('Mermaid' fountain, 'Rosamund's Well', water parterre and cascade.)

Buscot Park (NT), Buscot, Faringdon SN7 8BU. Telephone: 01367 240786. Website: www.buscot-park.com (Mughal garden by Harold Peto, 'Mercury' pool, 'Satyr' fountain and man-made cascade.)

Greys Court Gardens (NT), Rotherfield Greys, Henley-on-Thames RG9 4PG. Telephone: 01494 755564. (Dutch stone fountain.)

Rousham House (PO), near Steeple Aston, Bicester OX25 4QX. Telephone: 01869 347110. Website: www.rousham.org (Rill from the octagonal pond in Venus' Vale to the cold bath.)

This nineteenth-century Italian copy of the bronze satyr with a wineskin, known from Pompeii before AD 79, is in the walled garden at Buscot Park. The satyr stoops to watch the jet spray from the wineskin.

Shropshire
The Museum of Iron, Ironbridge, Telford TF8 7AW. Telephone: 01952 433522. Website: www.ironbridge.org.uk ('Boy with a Swan' fountain.)
Weston Park (HHA), Weston-under-Lizard, near Shifnal TF11 8LE. Telephone: 01952 852100. Website: www.weston-park.com ('Putti' fountain.)

Somerset
Roman Baths and Pump Room (LA), Stall Street, Bath BA1 1LZ. Telephone: 01225 477785. Website: www.romanbaths.co.uk
Vivary Park, Upper High Street, Taunton. (Fountain by Macfarlane & Company, 1907.)
Weston-super-Mare: Clarendon Road South, centre of the park. ('Putti' fountain, 1970.)
Weston-super-Mare: The Italian Gardens, High Street. (Circular spray fountain, 1970.)

Staffordshire
Shugborough Hall (NT), Milford, Stafford ST17 0XB. Telephone: 01889 881388. Website: www.staffordshire.gov.uk ('Standing Boy and Swan' fountain.)
Walsall: Civic Square. ('Source of Ingenuity', a bronze washdown fountain by Tom Lomax, 2001.)

Suffolk
Shrubland Park Gardens (PO), Coddenham, Ipswich IP6 9QQ. Telephone: 01473 830221. Website: www.shrublandpark.co.uk (Natural water garden.)

Surrey
Royal Horticultural Society Gardens, Wisley, near Woking GU23 6QB. Telephone: 01483 224234. Website: www.rhs.org.uk (Formal canal; water features and fountains in the Model Gardens, the Eros Garden, the Daily Telegraph Reflective Garden and the Country Garden bubble-jet fountain.)

Sussex
Brighton: Old Steine. (Victorian cast-iron 'Dolphin' fountain designed by A. H. Wilds, 1846.)
Horsham Town Centre. ('Cosmic Cycle' fountain by Angela Conner, 2001.)
Nymans Garden (NT), Handcross, Haywards Heath RH17 6EB. Telephone: 01444 400321. (Fountains in compartment gardens.)
Pashley Manor Gardens (HHA), Ticehurst, Wadhurst TN5 7HE. Telephone: 01580 200888. Website: www.pashleymanorgardens.com (Fountains and springs.)

Warwickshire
Bancroft Gardens, Stratford-upon-Avon. ('Country Arts' fountain in marble and steel by Christine Lee, 1996.)
Birmingham: Centenary Square. ('Spirit of Enterprise' fountain by Tom Lomax.)
Birmingham: Victoria Square. ('The River' fountain by Dhruva Mistry.)
Caldecott Park, Evreux Way, Rugby. ('Princess Diana Memorial' fountain, 1997–9.)
Jephson Gardens, Leamington Spa. ('Hitchman' fountain.)
Nuneaton: junction of Newton Road and Corporation Street. ('Dandelion' fountain.)
Ragley Hall (HHA), Alcester B49 5NJ. Telephone: 01789 762090. Website: www.ragleyhall.com (Fountain in the rose garden.)
University of Aston in Birmingham, Aston Triangle, Gosta Green, Birmingham B4 7DU. Website: www.williampye.com ('Tipping Triangles' fountain by Angela Conner, 1994, and 'Peace' fountain by William Pye, 1985, in the lake between the halls of residence.)
University of Birmingham, Edgbaston Park Road, Birmingham B15 2TT. Website:

www.bham.ac.uk ('Mermaid' fountain, students' union building, by William Bloye, 1961.)

Wiltshire
Shute House (PO), Donhead St Mary, Shaftesbury SP7 9DG. Telephone contact: 01935 814389. (Water rills, formal pools and bubble fountains by Geoffrey Jellicoe.)
Stourhead (NT), Stourton, near Warminster BA12 6QD. Telephone: 01747 841152. (Sleeping nymph and river god in the grotto.)
Wilton House (HHA), Wilton, near Salisbury SP2 0BJ. Telephone: 01722 746720. Website: www.wiltonhouse.com (Two fountains, 1975 and 2000.)

Worcestershire
Bellevue Island, Great Malvern. (Two fountains by Rose Garrard: 'Malhvina', a bronze drinking fountain from 1998, provides a continuous supply of Malvern spring water from the hills; the 'Enigma' fountain in Portland stone and slate, from 2000, features a life-size figure of the composer Elgar.)
Witley Court (EH), Great Witley, Worcester WR6 6JT. Telephone: 01299 896636. ('Perseus and Andromeda' fountain, 'Flora' fountain [NW].)

Yorkshire – North
Castle Howard (HHA), York YO60 7DA. Telephone: 01653 648444. Website: www.castlehoward.co.uk ('Atlas fountain', 'Prince of Wales' fountain and cascade.)
The Forbidden Corner (PO), Tupgill Park Estate, Coverdale, Middleham, Leyburn DL8 4TJ. Telephone: 01969 640638. Website: www.yorkshirenet.co.uk/forbiddencorner (Twentieth-century folly garden with laser-activated trick fountains.)
Fountains Abbey and Studley Royal (NT), Ripon HG4 3DY. Telephone: 01765 608888. Website: www.fountainsabbey.org.uk (Moon pools, canal, cascade and lake.)
Newby Hall (HHA), Ripon HG4 5AE. Telephone: 01423 322583. Website: www.newbyhall.com (Compartment gardens with fountains.)

Yorkshire – South
Sheffield Peace Gardens (LA), Pinstone Street, Sheffield. (Water plaza.)

Yorkshire – West
Bramham Park (HHA), Wetherby LS23 6ND. Telephone: 01937 846000. Website: www.bramhampark.co.uk (Shaped water pools, cascade fountains.)
Eureka, the Museum for Children, Discovery Road, Halifax HX1 2NE. Telephone: 01422 330069. Website: www.eureka.gov.uk (Multi-cup steel tipping fountain that strikes musical tones as the cups empty.)
Harewood House (Charitable trust), Harewood, Leeds LS17 9LQ. Telephone: 0113 218 1010. Website: www.harewood.org ('Triton' fountains, 'Orpheus' water feature, terracotta 'Dolphin' fountain and cascade.)
Lister Park (LA), Bradford BD9 4NA. Telephone: 01274 751535. (Mughal gardens.)
People's Park (LA), off Hopwood Lane, Halifax. (Figure fountain and loggia with water masks.)

SCOTLAND
Alexandra Park, 671 Alexandra Parade, Glasgow G31. (The 'Saracen' fountain.)
Crathes Castle, Garden and Estate (NTS), Banchory AB31 5QJ. Telephone: 01330 844525. ('Boy with a Dolphin' and 'Boy with a Tortoise'.)
Culzean Castle and Country Park (NTS), Maybole KA19 8LE. Telephone: 01655 884455. Website: www.culzeancastle.net ('Triton' fountain.)
Glasgow Green, Glasgow G1. (The 'Doulton' fountain, undergoing restoration in 2004, to be

This rill in the Peace Gardens in Sheffield shows ceramic inlays of willow leaves. The underground plant room in the Peace Gardens controls the water-supply tank feeding the central jets beyond the rill and the fibre-optic lighting. The area promotes the interaction and relaxation of visitors.

re-sited in front of the People's Palace [see www.hathernware.com].)

The Great Garden of Pitmedden (NTS), Pitmedden Village, Ellon AB41 7PD. Telephone: 01651 842352. (Fountain in the parterre.)

Greenbank Garden (NTS), Flenders Road, Clarkston, Glasgow G76 8RB. Telephone: 0141 639 3281. Website: www.nts.org.uk (Pool and bronze water nymph entitled 'Foam'.)

Kelvingrove Park, Sauchiehall Street, Glasgow G3. ('Stewart Memorial' fountain by J. Mossman and J. Young, 1872. Undergoing restoration in 2004.)

Linlithgow Palace (HS), Linlithgow EH49 7AL. Telephone: 01506 842896. Website: www.historic-scotland.gov.uk (Fountain undergoing restoration in 2004.)

Princes Street Gardens (LA), Princes Street, Edinburgh EH1. (The 'Ross' fountain, west of the Mound.)

Scone Palace (HHA), Perth PH2 6BD. Telephone: 01738 552300. Website: www.scone-palace.co.uk ('Arethusa' fountain in the maze.)

WALES

Bodrhyddan (PO), Rhuddlan, Denbighshire LL18 5SB. Telephone: 01745 590414. Website: www.bodrhyddan.co.uk (Fountain on the parterre.)

City Hall (LA), Cathays Park, Cardiff CF10 3ND. ('Prince of Wales' fountain.)

Dyffryn Gardens (LA), St Nicholas, Cardiff CF5 6SU. Telephone: 029 2059 3328. Website: www.dyffryngardens.org.uk (Pompeian fountain, 'Dragon' fountain, reflecting pool and cascade.)

The National Botanic Garden of Wales, Llanarthne, Carmarthenshire SA32 8HG. Telephone: 01558 668768. Website: www.gardenofwales.org.uk (Fountains and rill.)

Powis Castle and Garden (NT), near Welshpool, Powys SY21 8RF. Telephone: 01938 551920. (Cyclix fountain.)

The Earls of Massereene created Antrim Castle gardens
between 1680 and 1715 in the style of Le Nôtre. The
lower part of the canal has an offshoot probably used to
moor punts to maintain a clear view along the canal. A
limestone cascade was added in Victorian times to
extend the northern section of the canal.

IRELAND

Antrim Castle Gardens (LA), Ranaldstown
Road, Antrim, County Antrim BT41 4LH.
Telephone: 028 9442 8000. (Canal with
Victorian cascade.)

Bantry House and Gardens (PO), Bantry,
County Cork. Telephone: +353 (0)27 50047.
Website: www.bantryhouse.ie (Fountain in
the Wisteria Circle.)

Powerscourt Estate (PO), Enniskerry, County
Wicklow. Telephone: +353 (0)1 204 6000.
Website: www.powerscourt.ie ('Triton'
fountain in the lake.)

West Park, Dublin. ('Rolling Stones' by Angela Conner for Harcourt Developments.)

ITALY

Palazzo Vecchio, Piazza della Signoria, Florence. (Verrocchio's 'Boy with a Dolphin' fountain,
1480s.)

Perugia: 'Fontana Maggiore', Piazza Quattro Novembre. (Circular civic fountain by Nicola
Pisano, 1278.)

Villa Barbarigo Pizzoni Ardemani (PO), Valsanzebio di Galzignano, near Padua. (Fountains and
cascades including trick fountains, 1698–1717.)

Villa d'Este (SO), Piazza Trento, I, 1-00019, Tivoli, Rome. Telephone: +39 (0) 77 422070.
(Monumental cascades, water organ, rills and numerous fountains.)

Villa Demidoff, Via Bolognese, Pratolino. ('Appennino' fountain by Giambologna, 1579.)

Villa Medici at Castello (SO), Via di Castello, Castello,
Florence. Telephone: +39 (0) 55 454791. (Marble
'Hercules and Antaeus' fountain by Tribolo *c.*1543,
with a reproduction of Ammannati's bronze
sculpture 'Hercules and Antaeus' [original figures
from 1559–60 now displayed indoors at nearby Villa
Petraia]; 'Appennino' fountain by Ammannati,
1563–5; 'Grotto of the Animals' – trick fountains by
Ammannati and Giambologna, finished 1572.)

Villa Medici at Petraia (SO), Via Della Petraia,
Castello, Florence. Telephone: +39 (0) 55 452691.
(Marble 'Fountain of Florence' by Tribolo, *c.*1545
[originally at Castello] and reproduction of
Giambologna's bronze figure of 'Florence' [original
figure of 'Florence', 1572, now displayed indoors].)

At Shute House in Wiltshire, water bubbles along this rill,
designed by Geoffrey Jellicoe in 1972, and over copper chevrons
on each cascade to produce different musical tones. The water
flow over the cascades resembles diving fishtails.

Acknowledgements

Thanks mainly to my husband, Geoff, for his support and encouragement, and to the following for their interest and help with this book: Allsebrook Pump Services; Antony House, Liz Luck; Antrim Castle Gardens, Philip Magennis; Athelhampton, Patrick Cooke; Barbican (Engineering), Frank Woods; Battersea Park, Jennifer Ullman; Blenheim Palace, His Grace the Duke of Marlborough; Bolsover Castle, Andrea Buckingham; Bramham Park, Claudia Langmead and Patrick James, The Landscape Agency; Buscot Park, Lord Faringdon; Castle Howard, The Honourable Simon Howard; Chatsworth House, Peter Day; Cheltenham Museum, Dr Stephen Blake; Cliveden, Graham Deans; Angela Conner; Angela Conner's photographs, John Bulmer; Crescent Lighting Limited, Alan Weaver; Crystal Palace Museum, Melvyn Harrison; Culzean Castle, Gordon Riddle; Dunorlan fountain, Claude Hitching (Pulhamite); Dunorlan Park, Ian Beavish, Tunbridge Wells Library (Kent Arts and Libraries); Edinburgh City Council, Dorothy Marsh; Exbury Gardens, Victoria Martin; Farleigh House, the Countess of Portsmouth; Forbidden Corner, Malcolm Tempest; Fountain Society, Peter Knowlson; Glasgow School of Art, Ray McKenzie; Haddonstone Limited, Simon Scott; Hampton Court, Leominster, Simon Dorrell; Hampton Court Palace, Suzanne Groom; Harewood House, Karen Lynch; Hathernware, Geoff Hollis; Hever Castle, Ann Watt; Holkham Hall, Christine Hickey and Colin Shearer; Ironbridge Gorge Museum, John Powell; Kiftsgate Court, Mr and Mrs Chambers; Lafarge Company (Cement), Ian Heritage; Linlithgow, Nick Bridgeland; Lister Park, Bradford, David Elcock; Tom Lomax; Manchester, Mike Pilkington; Manchester Piccadilly, Matt Cawley (City Council) and Warren Osborne (EDAW); Barry Mason; Melbourne Hall, Lord Ralph Kerr; Newby Hall, Philippa Walton; Nuneaton, Richard Cook; Painswick, Paul Moir; Pitmedden, Susan Burgess; William Pye; Ritchie MacKenzie Company Limited, Alnwick, Paul Mitchell; Roman Baths Museum, Susan Fox; Royal Academy of Arts, Burlington House, Peter Schmitt; Royal Brompton Hospital, Dr Philip Kilner; Royal Parks, Greg McErlean and Jason Dudley-Mallick; Scone Palace, David Williams-Ellis; Sheffield, Rick Bingham; Shrubland Park, Lord de Saumarez; Shute House, Andrew Lawson; Somerset House, Edward Schofield; Stanway, Lord Neidpath; Stourhead, Katharine Boyd; Studley Royal, Joanne Hassall; Thames Barrier Park, David Calvert (and Martin Charles for the photograph); Philip Thomason, Thomason Cudworth; Torsion, London, Geoff Wallis and Dorothea Restorations; University of Leeds, Dr Joseph Holden; Ustigate Limited, Jeremy Sutherland; Victoria and Albert Museum, Dr Peta Motture; Wales Botanic Gardens, Anthony Jellard Associates; West Wycombe Park, Tim Knox; Westminster Archives, Llinos Thomas; Westminster Council, Dominic Strickland; Alan Wilson; Wilton House, R. W. Steadman; Winchester, Corporation Graphics of Hampshire County Council, John Woodhead; Witley Court, Brian Powell & Company; The Dean and Chapter of Westminster.

The photographs on pages 1, 3, 4, 6 (both), 7 (all), 8 (top), 9 (top), 10 (bottom), 12 (bottom), 13 (bottom), 14 (both), 15 (both), 16 (all), 17 (both), 18 (top), 19 (top), 20 (all), 21, 22 (both), 24 (top and bottom), 27, 28 (both), 31 (both), 34 (both), 35 (top and bottom right), 36 (top), 37 (top two), 38 (both), 39 (top and centre), 40 (top and centre), 41 (all), 42 (centre), 45 (top), 47 (bottom right), 48 (all), 49 (top and centre), 50 (top), 51, 55 (top and bottom), 58 (top and bottom) were taken by the author. Other illustrations are acknowledged as follows: Anthony Jellard Associates, page 49 (bottom); Antrim Borough Council, page 62 (top); Birmingham City Council, page 47 (top and bottom left); The British Library, IB2449, page 10 (top), Hirsch I. 108. (1), page 13 (top); John Bulmer, pages 37 (bottom), 43 (top); Buscot Park, pages 36 (top), 58 (bottom); Mr and Mrs J. G. Chambers, pages 3, 7 (top); Martin Charles, page 40 (bottom); Cheltenham Borough Council, page 32 (top); the City of Edinburgh Council, page 25 (top); Patrick Cooke, page 26 (bottom); Corporation Graphics of Hampshire County Council, page 8 (top); Crescent Lighting Limited, page 45 (centre and bottom); the Dean and Chapter of Westminster, page 51; Dorothea Restorations Limited, page 43 (bottom); English Heritage, pages 14 (left), 27; Fountains Abbey, page 19 (top); Harewood House Trust, pages 20 (centre), 35 (bottom right); Hever Castle Limited, pages 33, 36 (centre); Crown Copyright, reproduced courtesy of Historic Scotland, page 11 (top); Geoff Hollis, page 30 (bottom); Ironbridge Gorge Museum Trust, pages 23 (bottom), 24 (centre); Dr Philip Kilner, page 44 (bottom); Mr N. Lane Fox, page 18 (both); Andrew Lawson, page 62 (bottom); Robert J. Leighton, page 36 (bottom); the London Illustrated News Picture Library, page 23 (top); Lord Wemyss Trust, page 19 (bottom); Ray MacKenzie, page 25 (centre); Manchester City Council, pages 25 (bottom), 46 (bottom); by kind permission of His Grace the Duke of Marlborough, pages 7 (bottom), 58 (top); Melbourne Garden Charitable Trustees, page 17 (bottom); the National Trust, pages 1, 19 (top), 20 (top), 28 (both), 35 (bottom left); the National Trust for Scotland, pages 12 (top), 29 (top); the National Trust, Stourhead, page 21; Nuneaton and Bedworth Borough Council, page 44 (centre); William Pye, page 42 (top and bottom); RIBA Library Photographs, page 12 (top); © The Royal Parks, page 50 (bottom); Sheffield City Council Photography Unit, pages 46 (top), 61; Somerset House Trust, page 39 (bottom); Philip Thomason, page 29 (bottom); Trustees of Wilton House Trust, pages 34 (bottom), 35 (top); Tunbridge Wells Library: Kent Arts & Libraries, page 30 (top); V&A Picture Library, page 8 (bottom); Waddesdon Manor, page 28 (top); G. J. O. Wallis, page 43 (bottom); Alan Wilson, page 44 (top).

Permission to use Grid References from the London A–Z index is given by the Geographer's A–Z Map Company Limited.

Index